Anir
T0080782

Bird Body Parts

Clare Lewis

heinemann raintree

© 2016 Heinemann-Raintree
an imprint of Capstone Global Library, LLC
Chicago, Illinois

To contact Capstone Global Library please call 800-747-4992, or visit our web site www.capstonepub.com

All rights reserved. No part of this publication may be reproduced or transmitted in any form or by any means, electronic or mechanical, including photocopying, recording, taping, or any information storage and retrieval system, without permission in writing from the publisher.

Edited by Helen Cox Cannons and Shelly Lyons
Designed by Steve Mead
Picture research by Svetlana Zhurkin
Production by Victoria Fitzgerald
Originated by Capstone Global Library Ltd

Library of Congress Cataloging-in-Publication Data
Lewis, Clare, 1976- author.
Bird body parts / Clare Lewis.
pages cm.—(Animal body parts)
Includes bibliographical references and index.
ISBN 978-1-4846-2553-8 (hb)—ISBN 978-1-4846-2560-6 (pb)—ISBN 978-1-4846-2574-3 (ebook) 1. Birds—Anatomy—Juvenile literature. I. Title.

QL697.L49 2016
598—dc23 2014044029

This book has been officially leveled by using the F&P Text Level Gradient™ Leveling System.

Acknowledgments
We would like to thank the following for permission to reproduce photographs: Dreamstime: Mario Madrona Barrera, 12, Martin Ellis, 16, Matthewgsimpson, 22 (middle), Physi28, 22 (top), Rhallam, 17, 23; iStockphoto: John Carnemolla, 9; Shutterstock: Andreas Gradin, 8, Andrey Feodorov, cover (top middle), Bildagentur Zoonar GmbH, 7, bofotolux, 21, Chet Mitchell, 22 (bottom), Christian Musat, back cover (left), 15, 23, Cucumber Images, 18, EBFoto, 10, Eduard Kyslynskyy, 6, 23, Gallinago_media, 19, hfuchs, 11, Jack Ammit, cover (bottom), Neil Bradfield, 5, ODM Studio, back cover (right), 20, 23, Oleg Elena Tovkach, cover (top left), Philip Hunton, 13, 23, SantiPhotoSS, 4, 23, Steffen Foerster, cover (top right), Tobie Oosthuizen, 14.

We would like to thank Michael Bright for his invaluable help in the preparation of this book.

Every effort has been made to contact copyright holders of material reproduced in this book. Any omissions will be rectified in subsequent printings if notice is given to the publisher.

All the Internet addresses (URLs) given in this book were valid at the time of going to press. However, due to the dynamic nature of the Internet, some addresses may have changed, or sites may have changed or ceased to exist since publication. While the author and publisher regret any inconvenience this may cause readers, no responsibility for any such changes can be accepted by either the author or the publisher.

Printed in the United States 5038

Contents

What Is a Bird? **4**
Eyes **6**
Ears and Nostrils **8**
Beaks **10**
Feathers **12**
Wings **14**
Tails **16**
Legs **18**
Feet **20**
Totally Amazing Bird Body Parts! **22**
Glossary ***23***
Find Out More ***24***
Index ***24***

Some words are shown in bold, **like this**. You can find out what they mean by looking in the glossary.

What Is a Bird?

Birds have feathers and beaks. They lay eggs. They have a backbone and wings.

Robins, flamingos, and parrots are birds. Penguins are birds, too.

Birds do not all look the same. Their bodies can be very different from each other.

Let's take a look at parts of their bodies.

Eyes

Some birds have large eyes.

Owls' eyes help them see their **prey** at night. They need to see well at night because most owls are **nocturnal**.

Some birds, like this pheasant, have eyes on the sides of their heads. This helps them to watch out for danger all around them.

Ears and Nostrils

Most birds can hear very well.

Their ear holes are usually hidden under their feathers. It can be difficult to see the hidden ear holes.

Birds have nostrils near the bottom of their beaks. Many birds cannot smell very well.

However, kiwis can smell well. They sniff for worms and snails hidden in the earth.

Beaks

All birds have beaks.

Many birds of prey, such as this vulture, have hooked beaks. Its hooked beak is sharp, for tearing meat.

Woodpeckers have sharp, straight beaks.

They use their beaks to make holes in trees and find tasty bugs to eat.

Feathers

Some birds have very colorful feathers.

Male peacocks shake their beautiful tail feathers to attract a **mate**.

Sparrows have brown feathers.

Brown feathers help them to hide from **predators**.

Wings

Most birds use their two wings for flying.

This eagle uses its large wings to soar through the air. As it soars, it looks down to find animals to eat.

Some birds, such as emus, ostriches, and penguins, cannot fly.

Penguins use their wings like **flippers** to help them swim through water.

Tails

Some birds' tails are useful for flying. Their tails work with their wings to help them to lift off the ground.

Tails help birds to steer through the air.

Sparrowhawks have long tails.

Long tails help sparrowhawks to change direction quickly when chasing **prey**.

Legs

All birds have two legs.

Flamingos have very long legs. They can wade through water without getting their feathers wet.

Swifts have tiny legs and feet. They can hardly walk.

Swifts spend most of their lives flying. They can fly hundreds of miles in one day.

Feet

Birds of prey have large claws on their feet called **talons**.

Talons are good for catching and carrying their **prey**.

Many water birds, such as geese, swans, and ducks, have webbed feet.

Water birds use their webbed feet like paddles to help them swim.

Totally Amazing Bird Body Parts!

The bee hummingbird can beat its wings 200 times per second! The wings move so fast that they are a blur!

Ostriches are the tallest birds. They can run fast, but they cannot fly.

Pelicans have a special pouch under their beak. They can catch fish in their pouch.

Glossary

flipper wide, flat body part used to help animals swim

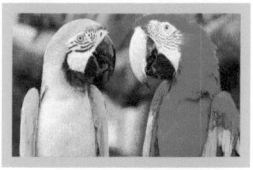

mate partner of an animal. Male animals look for female mates.

nocturnal active at night and asleep in the day

predator animal that hunts other animals for food

prey animal that is hunted by another animal

talon curved, sharp claw

Find Out More

Books

Gray, Susan Heinrichs. *The Life Cycle of Birds* (Life Cycles). Chicago: Heinemann Library, 2012.

Royston, Angela. *Birds* (Animal Classifications). Chicago: Heinemann Library, 2015.

Web sites

Facthound offers a safe, fun way to find Internet sites related to this book. All of the sites on Facthound have been researched by our staff.

Here's all you do:
Visit www.facthound.com
Type in this code: 9781484625538

Index

birds of prey 10, 20

eggs 4

nocturnal animals 6, 23

predators 13, 23

prey 6, 17, 20, 23

swimming 15, 21

talons 20, 23

webbed feet 21